Boaz, The Promise and the Wait

The Single Christian Woman's Survival Guide to Preparing for God-Ordained Marriage

TONIA SHALEL
The best-selling author of *My Beauty for Ashes*

Boaz, The Promise and the Wait, by Tonia Shalel
© Copyright 2018 by Tonia Shalel

Cover design © 2018 by Tonia Shalel

All rights reserved. No part of this book may be reproduced
or used in any manner without the express written permission
of the publisher except for the use of brief quotations
in a book review.

Editing by Paula Conliffe
ISBN: 978-0-9992457-0-5

Dedication

*I dedicate this book to my Boaz. You are God's choice,
the man he predestined for me before the foundation of the earth. I lift
you up in prayer daily and I also pray for the ministry of our marriage.
I know that our story will be a testimony that when you wait on God,
he will give you the desires of your heart. I love you babe!*

Acknowledgements

Jesus, my first love

I would like to give all honor, all praise, and all glory to my Lord and savior Jesus Christ. I cannot believe I am writing a second book, but once you gave me the title, book cover, and chapter outline, I said, "Ok Lord, here we go again, what do you want me to say?" I am simply amazed at your love, grace, mercy, and loving kindness towards me.
All I want to do is serve you with my life, draw others closer to you, and make you smile.
You are my everything and I love you!

Kayla Amaya

Kayla, my beautiful daughter, I am so proud of the young lady of God you are becoming. Every single day you inspire me. You have a heart of gold, a genuine love for people, and you are going to do great things in the Kingdom of God. Thank you for your patience and understanding as I serve God's people.
I love you princess!

Paula

Paula, I am so blessed to have you as my sister. Growing up as children, I always admired you and you are still my shero. You have been one of my biggest cheerleaders. As I walk out the purpose and destiny on my life, I am so grateful for all that you do. You are the best copy editor/proofreader and you are not afraid to tell me what you really think even if it's not my original plan. As I've shared the vision the Lord has given me for my life, not once have you questioned it but always encouraged me especially during this current season of relentless spiritual warfare. I know you will give me your honest feedback and I love you for it.
Thank you! I love you!!

Sherry Cain

What can I say sis? You are my sister from another mother. I am amazed at how the Lord brought us into each other's lives. God told us he would send us people who got it and he is not like man, he cannot lie! You are my purpose mate, my coach, my sister, my ride or die, and a blessing in my life. I am so grateful for you!!! Whether you are encouraging me as a friend or in your gentle sweet voice coaching me to get busy with our Daddy's business, you know what to say and how to say it. You have impacted my life in so many ways and inspire me every day to "boss up". I love you Sis! Thank you for blessing me with your presence in my life!!!

Jeniffer

My friend, what can I say about you? You were the catalyst for my being obedient in launching the ministry, beginning my journey of purpose, and walking with me during one of the most challenging seasons of my life. Thank you for speaking life over me. Thank you for pushing me and sharing what God tells you to share even if I am not ready to hear it. I love you dearly and cherish our friendship.

Thyra

Thank you for your selflessness and your transparency. I am so grateful for everything you poured into me and for your obedience to walk with me. I would not be the woman of God I am today without you. I love you my friend.

My Instagram Family

We started off as strangers and screen names, and ended up as friends. Your willingness to allow me a glimpse into your lives has blessed me so much. Thank you Carly Reid, Marie-Therese Pontasch, Marlene Downing, Alaina Denise, Mary Hodge, Latonya Freeman, Mya Kay, Kelly and Tara Hightower. Our fellowship through Instagram inspired many things I wrote about in this book.

My Ministry Brothers and Sisters in Christ

I appreciate each and every one of you: Coco Gayle, Natalie Diamond, Bridgett Banks, Shelley Meche'tte, Candy Javon, LaToya Moulton, Azie Hudson, Rachel Gilder, and Elrick Jones.

My Family and Friends

I thank you for your love and support in no particular order: Mommy, Daddy (RIP), Durell, Horace Jr., Charles, Jordan, Jason, Sherine, Shalonda, Denise Jackson, Reverend Kenneth Dean, Sharon Dean, Oscar, Denise Bell, Kalima, Pastor Wayne Chaney Jr, Myesha Chaney, all of my Antioch Church of Long Beach family, Erica and Michael Cox, and Hosie Thomas.

Table of Contents

Dedication i

Acknowledgements iii

Introduction (Every Little Girl's Dream) ix

In the Beginning *(God's Order)* 1

Who Am I Lord God? What's Purpose Got to Do With It? 7

Get Busy With Your Father's Business 19

Drown Out the Distractions 25

But God I'm Tired of Waiting for Boaz ... I Want Bae!! 31

Prepare for What You Pray for 37

Praying for Your Boaz 49

Prayer Journal 51

Reflections from the Author 59

About the Author 61

Introduction (Every Little Girl's Dream)

I remember it like it was just yesterday. It was the day I dreamed of being in that white dress, walking down the aisle looking at my handsome husband. If you are reading this book, then I assume you are very much like me and have a strong desire to be married. I have had this strong desire to be married since I was a little girl. God showed me that I would be married, but he didn't tell me when. Now, this has been hard for me growing up in our society. Let's be real, being single is often looked at as a disease. If you are not married by 30, with 2 kids there must be something wrong with you, right? You must have issues (Don't we all, Lol!) or be angry or hard to get along with. Beautiful woman of God, there is nothing wrong with you. Let me tell you that we have a timetable and God has a timetable. We cannot even begin to understand God's master plan. Growing up, I always thought my love story would mimic my sister's story. She met her husband during her freshman year of college, they fell in love, got great jobs, got married after college, had 2 babies, then bought a house. That's the perfect love story, that's the way it is supposed to be, right? Wrong, wrong, wrong, I finally discovered. God has a different plan and path for each of us.

God's word says that he will give us the desires of our hearts, but there is a time and a place – and a season. If we try to rush our season, we will become frustrated. Have you ever wondered how you navigate through this single season and how you maintain a holy lifestyle submitted to God? I decided to write this book because I believe it is needed. Here is my survival guide for the single Christian woman waiting on God-ordained marriage.

In the Beginning (God's Order)

Genesis 1:27

"So God created mankind in his own image, in the image of God he created them; male and female he created them."

First things first – you must understand that God is a God of order. Everything he does is purposeful and intentional. Operating in our flesh, we want what we want when we want it. God works on Kairos time – not Chronos time. Chronos time is chronological but means nothing to the God of the universe. God operates on Kairos time, which is his appointed time to act. At times, we may believe God is taking too long to answer our prayers. So we get impatient and try to take matters into our own hands.

Listen to me, I've been there, done that and it has always ended in disaster. Let me tell you from experience, don't do it!! Do not rush God's perfect timing. When you operate out of God's timing you may miss out on the blessings he has in store for you. I think it's testimony time!

Corporate America is a dark and evil place – trust me, I know. I will also tell you that Human Resources can be one of the most evil places to work. As a Human Resources professional, your ethical responsibility is to be an advocate for the employee while at the same time mitigating risk for the organization. It is a delicate balance, but it is what you are called to do. I would say the majority of the HR professionals I have worked with will always side with management. I have seen people lie, cover up, and do whatever they can to protect the company – often at the detriment of the employee. Jesus calls many of his children to corporate America because we are the light in the darkness.

Many years ago I worked at a company where there was definitely spiritual warfare at play. I know corporate America is ungodly, but this was on a whole other level. The mission statement and ideology of this company was in total opposition to the things of God. At one point, the leadership of the organization released a "Manifesto" which included daily meditation practices, pseudo Buddhist principles, and at one point a senior VP walked around ringing bells so we could stop and close our eyes. I can remember interviewing a candidate and being totally embarrassed. By the time I was laid off, I heard people were required to take a class where they bowed to a statue. As a disciple of Jesus, my spirit was very unsettled daily walking through the hallways. After returning from my maternity leave, the environment was worse than when I left. Everyone walked around with eyes to the ground, not making eye contact, and looking miserable. It was depressing and I wanted out in the worst way. After the first round of layoffs, I fervently began my job search. I kept sending out my resume for jobs I knew I was more than qualified for with not even a call back for a phone screen.

Now, I'm not tooting my own horn, but I had several years of experience in Human Resources, a Master's degree, and I worked in recruitment. I knew my resume was stellar and my experience was solid. However, God would not release me. God had me on assignment and my light was needed during those years. One of my co-workers and sisters-in-Christ said, "Tonia, until you speak up and do what God is telling you to do, he will not release you." I would sit in meeting after meeting where my colleagues would make decisions that only benefited management and were, for lack of a better word, heartless. There was no consideration for the employee. I began to speak up in all of the meetings. Now, I didn't have the power to change their minds or influence the final decision at the executive level, but I let it be known I thought the decisions were wrong. This is what I was required to do as a disciple of Jesus – speak up for what is right. This went on for 3 years. Then, it happened.

I got called into the office and was given my layoff notice. The next week I was interviewing. God set it up in his timing that I would have multiple interview opportunities, a 10-week working notice where I was able to interview during company time, and a 2-week vacation before I started my next job. He literally gave me exactly what I prayed for. Due to the economic downturn, I was expecting to take a pay cut. I canceled my Sprint cell-phone contract, got a less expensive phone, and created a budget of how I was going to live on unemployment and my severance package. Well, I put the awesome God that we serve in a box. Let me tell you how he showed up and showed out. He gave me a severance package, $8,000 increase in pay, 2-week vacation, and a trip to Hawaii with my final paycheck. I never had to file for unemployment because the job offer was made to me during my last week on the payroll.

Now, if God had given me what I wanted three years prior, I would not have had any of those blessings. I didn't understand and couldn't see what he was putting together behind the scenes. All I knew was that I was miserable at that company and I wanted him to release me. I did not understand that God is a God of order.

During creation, God created all animals and plants, in a specific order, but when he was done, he knew there was something missing. He created Adam, the first man in his own image. Adam had a purpose and a kingdom assignment. It was only after creating Adam that God saw that he needed a help meet and then he formed Eve from Adam's rib. Many of us simply don't understand God's order.

For a long time, I had it backwards. I thought that once I "found" my husband, everything would be perfect and fall into place. Well, I was all out of order. First, a woman does not find her husband. The bible says that a man that finds a wife, finds a good thing and obtains favor from the Lord. However, before a man can find his wife, he needs to understand who he is, and most importantly, must know his kingdom assignment. The first man, Adam, knew his assignment. God gave him his assignment.

Genesis 2:8-24

> *"The Lord God took the man and put him in the Garden of Eden to work it and take care of it. And the Lord God commanded the man, "You are free to eat from any tree in the garden; but you must not eat from the tree of the knowledge of good and evil, for when you eat from it, you will certainly die." The Lord God said, "It is not good for the man to be alone. I will make a helper suitable for him." Now the Lord God had formed out of the ground all the wild animals and all the birds in the sky. He brought them to the man to see what he would name them; and whatever the man called each*

living creature, that was its name. So the man gave names to all the livestock, the birds in the sky and all the wild animals. But for Adam, no suitable helper was found. So the Lord God caused the man to fall into a deep sleep; and while he was sleeping, he took one of the man's ribs and then closed up the place with flesh. Then the Lord God made a woman from the rib he had taken out of the man, and he brought her to the man.

The man said, "This is now bone of my bones and flesh of my flesh, she shall be called 'woman,' for she was taken out of man." That is why a man leaves his father and mother and is united to his wife, and they become one flesh."

Once God gave Adam his assignment, he was ready for his wife. If a man doesn't know who he is and doesn't understand his assignment, how will he know if you are his purpose partner? God is not random with anything. He brings people together for his purpose and his glory. The world has a very warped view of marriage. People meet, hook up, get together because of how the person makes them feel, and if it doesn't work out, they are on to the next. Marriage is serious business. It's a covenant between a husband, a wife, and God. It is nothing to play around with. Many Christians believe that marriage will make them feel complete, but that is untrue. Only a real relationship with Jesus will satisfy that longing in your soul. Until you know Jesus for real for real, then you won't know who you are and why you are here. Before he formed you in your mother's womb, he had a plan, purpose, and destiny for your life.

Jeremiah 29:11 New Living Translation (NLT)

[11] *"For I know the plans I have for you," says the LORD. "They are plans for good and not for disaster, to give you a future and a hope."*

If a man doesn't know his assignment, then he will not know you when he sees you.

Remember Adam was sleeping when God formed Eve out of his rib. However, when he was awakened, he said, "This is now bone of my bone and flesh of my flesh." How did Adam know that? He was sleeping. She was a part of him and he knew it instantly when he saw her. Adam knew his assignment, God presented his wife, and then he recognized her. Order, order, order – I cannot stress enough that God is a God of order. Now, as a woman waiting on God-ordained marriage, what must you understand about God's order?

Do you remember that song from Diana Ross from the movie "Mahogany?" Ok, I may be dating myself but as a little girl, that was one of my favorite songs. "Do you know where you're going to, do you know the things that life is showing you, where are you going to, do you know?" Ok, ladies, let me ask you something. Do you know who you are? You might think you do, but many of us are walking around praying for husbands, asking God to send us Boaz, and we don't even know who we are. If you don't truly know who you are, then how do you know who God has ordained for you? How will you recognize him when God presents him to you? No fear, I am here to show you how to survive this season of waiting.

Who Am I Lord God? What's Purpose Got to Do With It?

Romans 8:28

"And we know that all things work together for good to them that love God, to them who are the called according to his purpose."

I'm about to drop some knowledge on you – many of you ladies reading this book are not ready for your God-ordained husbands. Don't shoot the messenger sis, please! I know this is hard to read and believe me this is something I had to come to terms with myself. I didn't know who I truly was until 2016 at 40-something years of age. Year after year, relationship after relationship, I was just drifting looking for something and didn't realize I was completely lost. Before God formed you in your mother's womb, he knew you. God has gifted you with talents for his glory and for his kingdom. If you haven't identified the reason why you were born, you are not ready for marriage. What's purpose got to do with it ladies? In short, everything!!! Many of us are so focused on being married we don't slow down to spend time in God's face asking him, "Lord, why am I here?"

Survival Tip #1 – Seek God in order to discover your purpose

Ok, I know this sounds like a lot to take in but many of us are walking around totally dazed and confused. That was me – every day I was getting up going to work, picking up my daughter from school, watching reality television shows, dating the flavor of the year, going to church on Sundays, and that was it. God did not create his children to wander through life aimlessly. When you accept Christ as your Lord and savior and receive the Holy Spirit and begin your journey, one of the things many believers miss is purpose. I really didn't get it. I didn't really realize that God had an assignment for me, that only I could fulfill, and the longer I delayed discovering my purpose, there were people suffering. So, that sounds great Tonia, but how do I discover my purpose? I sincerely believe that the more we spend time with God, the more he will order our steps in the way we should go. Each of us has different talents and gifts the Lord blessed us with. We all need to understand our gifts in order to discover our purpose.

If you take some time to just reflect on your strengths and talents, that is a great starting point. In 2013, one of my friends launched a Facebook group that was reading **The Purpose Driven Life**. I had always been curious about that book and thought it would be interesting to read. Little did I know that the Lord was ordering my steps. I think this book is amazing and I think it is even more powerful when you read it with others. There are great discussion questions at the end of each chapter which require you to reflect. By the time I had finished the book with the group, many things had been confirmed and clarified for me.

Since I was a very little girl, I always had a great desire to help people. When I was 14 years old, I volunteered at a local hospital as a candy striper. I used to enjoy wheeling the patients around, helping the nurses, and seeing the patients' faces light up during my shift. At one point I thought about pursuing a nursing career, but I soon realized that wasn't going to work. I am scared of blood, needles, and I am very squeamish. However, the deep desire to help others was still there. So, instead of pursuing a nursing career, I decided to become a teacher instead. In my senior year of college during the student teaching phase of my teaching program, I felt alive. When my students finally got a concept or told me I helped them, it brought me so much joy. After graduation when I moved to California, I taught middle school for three years before I resigned. The stress of teaching was becoming way too much for me, but that desire to help people was still there. I started graduate school and then began my career in Human Resources as a recruiter, helping people find employment. Do you see the theme here? Although the job title and my career choice changed, the desire to help others never went away. That is because before God formed me in my mother's womb, he put that desire in my heart and it won't ever go away.

Ask yourself, when do you feel most alive? What is effortless for you to do that other people struggle with? Once I really took some time to reflect in that book club, I was able to identify my talents. I am what my friends call a "Super Project Planner on steroids."

I have since learned how to keep that in check, but I am very detailed oriented. When I was in high school, I started visiting the college office in my sophomore year and had a timeline 2 years in advance of the college application process. When I was in graduate school, I started writing my thesis a year before I defended it. I didn't even get approval on my topic but was so driven to start that I did anyway. Procrastination is not my thing. I can't stand last-minute things and I like to plan everything. You give me a project and a task, and I'm on it right away, ironing out all of the details way ahead of schedule.

During school and at work, I was always chosen to be the group leader or team leader because people knew I would get the job done. I realized that God gifted me with leadership abilities. Since I was a very little girl, I could not stop running my mouth. I am not shy at all, I can start a conversation with someone I don't know and keep going and going and going. Growing up, my teachers always commended me for my communication skills. I am not afraid to get up in front of large groups of people and speak. Public speaking is consistently identified as one of people's greatest fears. I realized God gifted me with strong communication abilities.

I have a desire to help, mentor, and encourage people. One of my spiritual gifts is the gift of encouragement. When any of my friends were feeling bad and needed to be encouraged, they would always call me. Ok, so you take all of these talents and abilities that God has given you and then what? How do you discover who God created you to be?

Believe me beautiful woman of God, if you continue to seek the Lord, he will order your steps. Once God started to give me a revelation about my gifts and talents through reading ***The Purpose Driven Life***, I should have sought him more but I didn't. Ladies, please don't make the same mistake

I did. I went back to becoming totally focused on finding my husband and abandoned what God was starting to show me. It wasn't until a wilderness season where my Daddy really dealt with me (I talk about this in my book, ***My Beauty for Ashes***) that I fully got it and discovered my true purpose.

In addition to reading the book and spending time with God, I also strongly suggest taking a spiritual gifts assessment. You can easily find one online and it really helps to identify your spiritual gifts. Once you take one step to show God you are serious, believe me, he will continue to reveal more and more about your purpose. Once I gave God my complete yes and started walking in my purpose, he continued to download daily in my spirit what to do next. The more you talk to him and seek him, the more clearly you can hear his voice.

What are Spiritual Gifts?

All believers who have accepted Jesus as their Lord and savior have been given at least one spiritual gift. Many believers have several spiritual gifts with some being more prominent. We find all of these spiritual gifts outlined in various passages of scripture, Romans 12:6-8, 1 Corinthians 12:8-10, 28-30, and Ephesians 4:11. I have listed all of the spiritual gifts below:

- Administration
- Knowledge
- Apostleship
- Leadership
- Discernment
- Mercy
- Evangelism

- Miracles
- Exhortation
- Pastor/Shepherd
- Faith
- Prophecy
- Giving
- Serving/Ministering
- Healing
- Teaching
- Interpretation of Tongues
- Tongues
- Wisdom

God has blessed me with 3 spiritual gifts, exhortation, faith, and serving/ministering. These 3 gifts all complement the work that God has currently called me to with respect to ministering to singles during their season of singleness. Each of these gifts builds on the other and equips me to do the kingdom work God has assigned to me.

The spiritual gift of exhortation is often called the "gift of encouragement." The Greek word for this gift is Parakaleo. It means to beseech, exhort, call upon, to encourage, and to strengthen. One of the main purposes of exhortation is to remind people of the incredible work of God in Jesus Christ and the beauty of the salvation we have received. Paul commands Titus to utilize this gift in Titus1: 1-9.

Titus 1:1-9

Paul, a servant of God and an apostle of Jesus Christ to further the faith of God's elect and their knowledge of the truth that leads to godliness— in the hope of eternal life, which God, who does not lie, promised before the beginning of time, and which now at his appointed season he has brought to light through the preaching entrusted to me by the command of God our Savior, To Titus, my true son in our common faith: Grace and peace from God the Father and Christ Jesus our Savior.

Appointing Elders Who Love What Is Good

The reason I left you in Crete was that you might put in order what was left unfinished and appoint elders in every town, as I directed you. An elder must be blameless, faithful to his wife, a man whose children believe and are not open to the charge of being wild and disobedient. Since an overseer manages God's household, he must be blameless—not overbearing, not quick-tempered, not given to drunkenness, not violent, not pursuing dishonest gain. Rather, he must be hospitable, one who loves what is good, who is self-controlled, upright, holy, and disciplined. He must hold firmly to the trustworthy message as it has been taught, so that he can encourage others by sound doctrine and refute those who oppose it.

Paul also charges Timothy with the same assignment in 2 Timothy 4:2.

2 Timothy 4:2

Preach the word; be prepared in season and out of season; correct, rebuke, and encourage—with great patience and careful instruction.

This gift of exhortation is given to the believer in order to uplift, edify, and strengthen those who are weary in their faith. The encourager's mission in the body of Christ is to continually edify their brothers and sisters in Christ for the glory of God. I never understood the importance of this gift until I launched my Instagram account. One of the challenges for believers is trying to overcome their own struggles and issues as they walk with the Lord. When someone is broken and has lost their faith, they understandably struggle with being able to do the work the Lord is calling them to.

When I think back to some of the issues my followers have shared with me, I realize how important this gift is to the body of Christ. I often put up posts on my social media encouraging my followers to direct message me their prayer requests. Usually I would get about 10 requests. At the end of the year in 2016 right before New Year's Eve, I put up a request and I had over 50 people respond. At one point I felt a little overwhelmed trying to respond to all of them because they came in all at once. As they started to share their prayer requests with me, I was humbled. Many shared that they were struggling with spouses who had abandoned them, depression, anxiety, suicidal thoughts, health issues, frustration with their singleness, finances, spirit of offense, battling sexual demons, and letting go of soul ties. As I read over many of these requests, I couldn't hold back the tears. Sometimes all someone needs is an encouraging word to strengthen their faith so that they don't give up.

Faith is the second spiritual gift the Lord has blessed me with as part of my kingdom assignment. My faith was developed during my walk with the Lord. When I gave my life over to the Lord in 2008 as an unwed pregnant woman with no family in California, I had faith that the Lord would provide for me and my daughter. The spiritual gift of faith is grounded in the unwavering certainty, assurance, and conviction where you live boldly for God demonstrating that faith in powerful ways. The Holy Spirit bestows the gift of faith to believers who will encourage and edify the body of Christ that God is sovereign and faithful and good all the time. Those with this spiritual gift know that God will move and are not caught off guard when God answers the prayers of his people. This is best illustrated in Hebrews 11 which clearly summarizes God's faithfulness for Abel, for Enoch, for Noah, for Abraham, and for Sarah.

Hebrews 11:1-13

"Now faith is confidence in what we hope for and assurance about what we do not see. This is what the ancients were commended for. By faith we understand that the universe was formed at God's command, so that what is seen was not made out of what was visible. By faith Abel brought God a better offering than Cain did. By faith he was commended as righteous, when God spoke well of his offerings. And by faith Abel still speaks, even though he is dead. By faith Enoch was taken from this life, so that he did not experience death: "He could not be found, because God had taken him away." For before he was taken, he was commended as one who pleased God. And without faith it is impossible to please God, because anyone who comes to him must believe that he exists and that he rewards those who earnestly seek him. By faith Noah, when warned about things not yet seen, in holy fear built an ark to save his family. By his faith he condemned the world and became heir of the righteousness that is in keeping with faith. By faith Abraham, when called to go to a place he would later receive as his inheritance, obeyed and went, even though he did not know where he was going. By faith he made his home in the promised land like a stranger in a foreign country; he lived in tents, as did Isaac and Jacob, who were heirs with him of the same promise. For he was looking forward to the city with foundations, whose architect and builder is God. And by faith even Sarah, who was past childbearing age, was enabled to bear children because she considered him faithful who had made the promise. And so from this one man, and he as good as dead, came descendants as numerous as the stars in the sky and as countless as the sand on the seashore. All these people were still living by faith when they died. They did not receive the things promised; they only saw them and welcomed them from a distance, admitting that they were foreigners and strangers on earth."

Service or ministering is the third spiritual gift the Holy Spirit has bestowed upon me. Ministry is act of service out of sincere love for the purposes of edifying the community of God's people. The intent is to empower the body of Christ to use their spiritual gifts and talents to their fullest potential. The gifts we are given are not for ourselves but for others. Ministering to others is the ability to look beyond oneself to reach out to the community. People with this gift are not looking to be acknowledged for their service but understand they are the vessel God is using to stand in the gap and to bring him glory. I didn't want anyone but close friends to know I had launched my online ministry. For a very long time there was no "face" to my social media pages. I was very comfortable posting with no one knowing what I looked like. One day God dealt with me about this and told me to record a thank you video to my followers following my wilderness season. I clearly heard from God but really didn't want to. He told me it was important for my followers to understand I was a "real person" so they could relate to me and open up to me more. I was very comfortable staying behind the scenes, but the Lord wasn't having it.

Reflection Questions

Ask those closest to you what they consider to be your greatest strengths.

What were some of your favorite subjects in school? What subjects did you get an "A" in consistently and you really didn't need to try that hard?

What things bring you the most joy?

Prayer

Father God, I come to you humbly – the one who knows my beginning, my middle, and my end. My deepest desire is to serve you Lord God and to serve your people. Please reveal to me the plans that you have for me. Please order my steps with divine kingdom connections, please show me how you want me to use my gifts and talents to glorify you Lord God. I know that my gifts are not for me but for the kingdom. I give you all the honor and the praise and thank you in advance for what you are going to do through me Lord God. In Jesus' name, Amen.

Get Busy With Your Father's Business

Luke 2:49

And He said to them, "Why did you seek Me? Did you not know that I must be about my Father's business?"

Ok, beautiful woman of God, ask yourself honestly, can you say you are on the mission about your Father's business? Be honest, what is your first thought, your frequent thought, and your fixed thought? When you wake up in the morning, what is the first thing you do, besides think about a cup of coffee? I'm going to tell you – before God dealt with me in my wilderness season, my first thought was whether the guy I was dating at the time had sent me a goodnight text, looking at Facebook or Instagram or concerning myself with other meaningless things. When I open my eyes in the morning now the first words I utter are, "Thank you Lord God, thank you for waking me up." It is something we take for granted, don't we? The alarm clock goes off and we hear it. However, at that exact moment, there are so many people who don't hear it because their life is over.

Once God had me in alignment, I would start my day with a spirit of gratitude, reading his Word, praying for my followers, and then asking him to use me as his vessel. Since I realized my purpose and assignment, not one day has gone by where I haven't done something related to my Father's business. I've got my secular job Monday through Friday and my sacred job. My sacred job is 24/7; there are no days off as a disciple of Jesus.

Survival Tip #2 – Get busy with your Father's business RIGHT NOW!

Once I received my marching orders from God in 2016, I was so busy I didn't have time to obsess about my future husband. Once I fully surrendered my will to him, it was one thing after another. Speaking from personal experience, many of us are driven to distraction with things that don't matter to God. I would spend hours scrolling through friends' timelines on Facebook, sharing the same video that had been shared countless times and God said to me, "Does your Facebook page glorify me Tonia, what are you doing?" All the time I wasted on there was distracting me from what he was calling me to do. Now, when I finally gave God my complete yes and cut it out, I could hardly keep up with everything he told me to do. One day I was on my lunch hour and he just started speaking to me so fast I had to rush and get a pen and paper so I could capture everything. He told me to find a photographer and get some professional photographs taken, commission a graphic artist to get my logo done, hire someone to design my business cards, complete my life coach certification, hire a website designer and get this all completed quickly. He said all of these things to me in July of 2016 and told me I had to get everything done by September. I didn't understand everything, but I knew I had to be obedient. I especially didn't understand the specific deadlines he was giving me.

One day a ministry reached out and wanted to collaborate with my ministry (Ruth and Boaz in the Meantime Ministries) on a conference call. They asked if I could send over my headshot for the flyer so they could start promoting the call. Well, I didn't have a professional headshot, so I had to do the best I could with some of my own pictures. Now, I got it. God was starting to line up opportunities and divine kingdom connections very quickly and I needed to get my business in order to be prepared when they reached out to me. Once God took me to the next level, there was no time for distraction.

After I said yes to God, he continued to order my steps and opened door after door after door. Ministries were contacting me to collaborate and I was being asked to be a guest on various podcast shows, live shows, and calls. God wanted me to open up my mouth, share my testimony, and encourage his people. All of a sudden I was so busy with all these things he was telling me to do that I had no time to obsess about my future husband. When you discover the reason why you were born it is the most amazing feeling in the world. Everything makes sense and you realize that it's not about you.

I remember when I realized I had to get the professional photos taken, I had to get a budget together, research studios, research photographers, research makeup artists, and become my own stylist because I had a very limited budget. I enlisted the help of two amazing friends. One of my friends has a photography business on the side and blessed me with her services for free. All I had to do was book the studio time. My other friend served as my stylist, assistant, and babysitter the day of the photo-shoot. All of the planning involved for the months and weeks leading up to the photo-shoot consumed a lot of my energy and time. However, this wasn't a frustrating type of busy because I was so happy and fulfilled. I honestly was not thinking about a relationship, marriage or my future husband.

When you are consumed with the things of God, your priorities shift. He begins ordering your steps and you are so in the "Yes God" flow that your purpose and assignment become the most important thing to you. When you align your will with the will of the Father, amazing things happen. Two weeks before the photo-shoot, the Lord also confirmed for me multiple times that he wanted me to write a book, my personal testimony (**My Beauty for Ashes**), and he told me that the book had to be finished in December and published by March 2017. So, I was juggling ministry collaborations, finishing my life coach certification program, planning for a photo-shoot, collaborating with the web designer for my website, and now I had to begin writing the book. This was in addition to commitments at church, my full-time job, and being a single Mommy. I was so incredibly busy and so on fire for what God was telling me to do. I had to create a project plan to stay on top of everything, but there wasn't one moment when I said, "This is too much God." You know when you are in God's perfect will, when you can't wait to do what he's telling you to do, when your heart smiles and your soul is so at peace. I had also mastered the importance of drowning out the distractions. Get ready to learn this very important principle in order to survive the season of waiting.

Reflection Questions

Have I set aside dedicated time daily to commune with my heavenly Father?

_____
_____
_____
_____
_____

On a scale of 1 to 10, how would I rate my prayer life?

_____
_____
_____
_____
_____

What action steps can I take today to begin seeking God to order my steps towards my purpose?

_____
_____
_____
_____
_____
_____

Prayer

Father God, I come to you earnestly seeking your will for my life. I know that as your Word says you have wonderful plans not to harm me but to give me hope and a future. I know that I need to get busy with your business. Please help me to stay focused on you, please direct me in the way I should go. In Jesus' name I pray, Amen.

Drown Out the Distractions

Colossians 2:8

"See to it that no one takes you captive by philosophy and empty deceit, according to human tradition, according to the elemental spirits of the world, and not according to Christ."

<u>*Survival Tip #3 – Get out of DRIVEN to DISTRACTION MODE now!*</u>

One of the tricks of the enemy is to distract you. He hates the call and destiny God has for you and he will stop at nothing to get you to fall into the routine of distraction, distraction, distraction. Be honest, how much time do you spend on things that are simply not important?

I had to really be honest with myself about how distracted I was. I would spend hours on the weekend watching every Real Housewives and Love and Hip Hop show while scrolling through my Facebook timeline. I was extremely distracted. You have an important kingdom assignment and God wants to use you, but you must allow the distractions to fall away. When you get busy with the things of God, your appetite will change. I was a reality television junkie, I watched every single ratchet show out there. Now, I have zero interest.

I would much rather be writing, encouraging, and ministering to a brother or sister in Christ who needs a word from God.

Another way we become distracted is when we focus on what others are doing. I always say, "Stay in your lane." Many of us are so preoccupied with what is going on in other people's lives, we completely miss the mark on what God is calling us to do in our own lives. That's one of the trappings of social media. Many people spend hours and hours thumbing through everyone's social media pages looking at what they are doing. It's a trick! God has work for you to do in the body of Christ. Let's consider the scripture about the two sisters Mary and Martha. Instead of focusing on Jesus' teaching, she was so caught up in what her sister wasn't doing and started whining to Jesus. Come on now Martha, get it together.

Luke 10: 38-42

"Now as they went on their way, Jesus entered a village. And a woman named Martha welcomed him into her house. And she had a sister called Mary, who sat at the Lord's feet and listened to his teaching. But Martha was distracted with much serving. And she went up to him and said, "Lord, do you not care that my sister has left me to serve alone? Tell her then to help me." But the Lord answered her, "Martha, Martha, you are anxious and troubled about many things, but one thing is necessary. Mary has chosen the good portion, which will not be taken away from her."

She interrupts Jesus with what isn't important to him to get him to bend to what's important to her. Do you want to be like Mary or do you want to be like Martha? Mary sat down at Jesus' feet, she wanted to hear from him, she wanted a Word from him. She knew she needed his wisdom. But, not Martha. Nope, Martha was so focused on trivial things she missed the opportunity to spend time at the Master's feet. Many of us are just like Martha – God may be trying to get our attention, but we are so caught up in our own desires we can't hear him clearly. When is the last time you sat down and listened? You have no peace in your soul and you have become obsessed with the need for immediate gratification.

In Matthew, Chapter 6, Jesus talks about how distracted we are with everyday life. Why do we worry about what we will eat, drink, or wear? The Lord will provide; worrying about these sorts of things is another huge distraction in our lives.

Matthew 6: 24-34

"No one can serve two masters, for either he will hate the one and love the other, or he will be devoted to the one and despise the other. You cannot serve God and money. "Therefore I tell you, do not be anxious about your life, what you will eat or what you will drink, nor about your body, what you will put on. Is not life more than food, and the body more than clothing? Look at the birds of the air: they neither sow nor reap nor gather into barns, and yet your heavenly Father feeds them. Are you not of more value than they? And which of you by being anxious can add a single hour to his span of life? And why are you anxious about clothing? Consider the lilies of the field, how they grow: they neither toil nor spin."

God reminds us that the flowers and the birds are not concerned about such things because of the Lord's provision. He has all of that under control. We must get our minds focused on the task at hand and get out of driven to distraction mode.

Many of us idolize marriage so much that we don't take the time to hear what "thus sayeth the Lord." If I had slowed down, and gotten in his face many years earlier, I wouldn't have wasted so much precious time obsessing about where my Boaz was. God had such important work for me to do, but I didn't take the time to be still enough to hear what he was saying to me. God was saying, "Yes Tonia, I heard your prayers, I know the desires of your heart because I placed them there, but I need you to get busy because I have important work for you to do – focus on me." When I think about all of the time I wasted, it truly grieves my spirit. I spent years and years and years trying to get God to adhere to my timetable about when I should be married instead of helping the people he has called me to minister to.

Social media can be both a blessing and a curse. Because of social media, I have been able to connect with thousands of people all over the world. This platform has allowed me to meet people I would have never met. Before my wilderness season, I spent countless hours on Facebook, scrolling, liking, commenting, and reposting. Yes, I had some ministries and pastors I was following, but most of the things I was doing was not glorifying God or anything related to the assignment he had for me. It was simply a distraction and a waste of my time. I would often say I didn't have time to pray or read my bible, but boy did I have time to waste on these social media sites. Once God dealt with me regarding this issue, he opened my eyes about social media. He showed me that the enemy has used social media to distract God's children. Most of us are just going about our daily routines and these sites are a huge distraction from the work God is calling us to. Now, as far as my Instagram, Facebook, Twitter and other sites, they are used to minister, encourage, edify, and uplift God's people. Another huge distraction for me was relationships with men that God did not send. We will talk more about that in the next chapter.

Reflection Questions

How do I spend my "free time" and how much of this time is spent watching television or scrolling through social media?

_____
_____
_____
_____
_____

How do I prioritize my time, ministry commitments, family, work, friends?

_____
_____
_____
_____
_____

How many hours do I have per week, per day, per month to focus on my purpose and kingdom assignment?

_____
_____
_____
_____
_____

Prayer

Lord God, I come to you humbly asking that you quiet the distractions in my life. I know that I have not always prioritized time with you and I ask that you forgive me. Please open my eyes and order my steps towards the things that you value and the work that you have for me. Please confirm for me your will Lord God. I want to focus on the things that are important to your kingdom Lord God. In Jesus' name I pray, Amen.

But God I'm Tired of Waiting for Boaz... I Want Bae!!

Matthew 15:8

"These people honor me with their lips, but their hearts are far from me."

<u>Survival Tip #4 – Don't be fooled by the Counterfeit!</u>

There is nothing on earth that can derail the purpose and destiny that God has for us more than a relationship that God did not ordain. Sis, I know, it's Friday night and you want to get up, get dressed, get cute, and go out on a date. Yes, I've been there so I can relate to how you are feeling. But, I can also tell you that dating the counterfeit Boaz is a distraction and a complete waste of your time. I think it's testimony time.

Many years ago I found myself in a relationship that God did not ordain. Well, that was the case with all of my relationships actually, but one in particular almost led to marriage. My ex-fiancé was very romantic, attentive, and loving. He called me his princess and spoiled me. Friday night was our date night and I used to love going home after work and changing into my cute date-night outfit. We would always go to a very nice restaurant and spend the evening holding hands and kissing. I felt so special. Well, what's wrong with that Tonia you might be saying – a girl needs love and attention, right? Well, sis, I will tell you what was wrong – God told me very early on that he was not the one.

God showed me the vision of my future husband very early on after my salvation in 2008. I was never able to see his face in the visions, but he showed me his character. He was a strong Godly man who knew his Word, could lead spiritually, was active in church and ministry, and was an excellent father. My ex-fiancé had none of these attributes. Simply put, I was settling because I wanted desperately to be married. He told me countless times to end it. But no, I was excited about the dress I had found at David's Bridal and I was excited about the hotel in Hawaii where we planned to have our destination wedding. I was envisioning my Facebook post when I would say, "I said yes!" with the ring he was designing for me. We were pre-registered for pre-marital counseling at a local church and I was forging ahead with my plan. Well, praise be to God, he blocked it. Sisters, God knows what he is doing. God was trying to tell me to end it on my own, but I didn't want to listen, so he ended it. I am so grateful to God that my destiny was so important to him that he shut down what would have been the biggest mistake of my life.

I am a woman who is on fire for God. The Lord is calling me to encourage and minister to his people. He knew I would launch a singles ministry, he knew I would be traveling to speaking engagements, and he knew I would write several books. Most importantly, he knew my ex fiancé would never be the man who could do life and ministry with me. My ex believed in Jesus and that was about it. He couldn't even pray for me. He was intimidated by anything related to Jesus and had not set foot in a church in 8 years when we started dating. He was trying to fit into shoes that he could never fill. The time I spent dating him and planning a wedding was a total waste of time. God brought him into my life for me to minister to him, not marry him.

The enemy hears your prayers to God and he knows what you want so he will send a counterfeit version of the blessing God has for you to take you off course. So, we hear so much about Boaz – wait on your Boaz. Well, exactly who was Boaz?

Ruth 2:5

"Boaz asked the overseer of his harvesters, "Who does that young woman belong to?" The overseer replied, "She is the Moabite who came back from Moab with Naomi. She said, 'Please let me glean and gather among the sheaves behind the harvesters.' She came into the field and has remained here from morning till now, except for a short rest in the shelter." So Boaz said to Ruth, "My daughter, listen to me. Don't go and glean in another field and don't go away from here. Stay here with the women who work for me. Watch the field where the men are harvesting, and follow along after the women. I have told the men not to lay a hand on you. And whenever you are thirsty, go and get a drink from the water jars the men have filled." At this, she bowed down with her face to the ground. She asked him, "Why have I found such favor in your eyes that you notice me—a foreigner?" Boaz replied, "I've been told all about what you have done for your mother-in-law since the death of your husband—how you left your father and mother and your homeland and came to live with a people you did not know before. May the Lord repay you for what you have done. May you be richly rewarded by the Lord, the God of Israel, under whose wings you have come to take refuge." "May I continue to find favor in your eyes, my lord," she said. "You have put me at ease by speaking kindly to your servant—though I do not have the standing of one of your servants."

Boaz was a noble man who blessed Ruth. He watched her working hard in the fields, inquired about her and came through with the major upgrade. Her life completely changed because of Boaz. Ruth stepped out on faith when she chose not to return to Moab and instead chose to go with her mother-in-law. Ruth could have continued grieving about the loss of her husband but instead she chose to serve and sacrifice. Your Boaz could be looking at you right now from afar. What is he going to see? Are you whining about being single or are you serving God and walking in your purpose?

Woman of God... will you know Boaz when you meet him? Have you prepared yourself? In the next chapter we will talk about the preparation process.

Reflection Questions

Am I content to wait on God or do I find myself dating just to date?

_____
_____
_____
_____
_____

Write down the characteristics of your future husband.

_____
_____
_____
_____
_____

Have the men you dated in the past possessed these characteristics?

_____
_____
_____
_____
_____

Prayer

Lord God, I come to you asking that you forgive me for my impatience. I acknowledge that I have often looked to others to fulfill what only you can. I know that a relationship with you is what my soul longs for and I ask that you grant me a spirit of patience. You know what is best for me. Help me to realize that jumping into another relationship not ordained by you will only lead to more pain. In Jesus' name I pray, Amen.

Prepare for What You Pray for

Proverbs 24:27

"Prepare your work outside; get everything ready for yourself in the field, and after that, build your house."

I hear many Christian single women saying that they are "waiting" for God to send them their husband. Waiting is passive – it means you are not moving, not growing, and not preparing. Preparation is key. In order to be successful in anything in life, you must prepare. When both people are ready to receive each other, then and only then will God make the introduction. Sis, let's be honest. If Boaz showed up at your door today, would you be ready to receive him? Let's take a look at Queen Esther from the bible.

Esther 2: 12-14

"Each young woman's turn came to go in to King Ahasuerus after she had completed twelve months' preparation, according to the regulations for the women, for thus were the days of their preparation apportioned: six months with oil of myrrh, and six months with perfumes and preparations for beautifying women. Thus prepared, each young woman went to the king, and she was given whatever she desired to take with her from the women's quarters to the king's palace. In the evening she went, and in the morning she returned to the second house of the women, to the custody of Shaashgaz, the king's eunuch who kept the concubines. She would not go into the king again unless the king delighted in her and called for her by name."

Queen Esther went through a one-year process in order to prepare for her king. She went through a beautification process of bathing herself in oils and perfumes. Beautification is a process of working on your mind, body, and spirit.

Have you started your beautification process? Have you worked on your health, woman of God? Many of us take a lot of time caring for our hair, makeup, and nails but don't take the time to work on our physical health. Our bodies are a temple of the Holy Spirit. We need to make sure we are caring for our temples and keeping it in the best shape we can.

What about your mind and spirit? Have you renewed your mind in terms of what it means to be a daughter of the king? You want a Godly man, but are you the Godly woman he is searching for? The world has a standard and God has a standard. I know it's easy to fall into the trappings of this world. Sex before marriage, shacking up, and jumping from relationship to relationship is not God's standard. We are to present our bodies as a sacrifice and honor our temples. That is his standard and if you want a man who is living by God's standards and you expect the Lord to bless you with a Boaz, you can't be a Jezebel or a Delilah sis, sorry – it doesn't work that way.

Revelations 2:20

"But I have this against you, that you tolerate that woman Jezebel, who calls herself a prophetess and is teaching and seducing my servants to practice sexual immorality and to eat food sacrificed to idols."

You are praying for God's best, but are you living a Godly lifestyle? Is your house in order? More importantly, have you thoroughly cleaned house? Ask yourself, have you dealt with all of the issues of your past, especially as it relates to past relationships? The majority of the survival tips are found in this chapter regarding preparation because there is a lot you must do to prepare yourself for God-ordained marriage.

Survival Tip #5 - Dump Your Baggage

Many of us are walking around completely broken. The truth is we don't know that we are broken. We truly believe we are healed, whole, and ready to be in a relationship. Trust me, I am speaking from my own experience. I am a recovered relationship junkie. Prior to salvation, I went from relationship to relationship hauling my emotional baggage that I had never dealt with. After giving my life to Christ in 2008, I still hadn't dealt with my brokenness and the emptiness I had from losing my father to cancer at age 9. So then, I carried that baggage with me from relationship to relationship with other believers (many who were also broken), looking for the man I was dating to fulfill that hole in my heart. Many of us are hauling a lot of baggage around.

Baggage is defined as past experiences or long-held ideas regarded as burdens or impediments. Baggage has a negative connotation because it drags you down and it weighs on your spirit. What kind of baggage do many women carry? We carry the baggage of the emotional scars of relationships that God never ordained for us. Out of a state of loneliness we often find ourselves accepting less than we deserve. Each failed relationship leaves us feeling disappointed which leads to feelings of insecurity. You start to believe there is something wrong with you, that you are not capable of experiencing true love.

Survival Tip #6 - Heal Your Heart

Woman of God, you must heal in order to be whole and ready for your husband. When there are unresolved issues in your heart such as bitterness, you can't be open to receive the love you deserve. For many of us, our hearts have been mishandled by people who didn't value us. Their callous treatment of our hearts caused a blockage. Just like those with a physical heart condition, our hearts can become clogged. Those who suffer from coronary disease have a build-up of plaque which causes a narrowing of the arteries. Those who suffer from a heart condition related to emotional heartbreak allow resentment, bitterness, unforgiveness, distrust, and anger to clog the pathway to our hearts. The Lord tells us in his Word to guard our hearts.

Proverbs 4:23

"Above all else, guard your heart, for everything you do flows from it."

The heart is at the center of everything we do. If your heart has been hardened by all of the baggage from your past relationships, how can you be open to receive love again? One of my friends used to say to me all the time she admired me for my open heart. No matter how many times I had been hurt, I knew that God had a wonderful love waiting for me. God told me my husband's heart was designed to love me and that our love will be supernatural. I never stopped believing that. However, even though my heart was open to receive love, there was still the residue of bad decisions and relationships that I had to work through. I never want my husband to have to pay for the way I was treated in my single season by other men. That is unfair to him.

My former pastor used to say all the time good marriages are made in your single season. An unhealthy single season is not setting you up for a healthy marriage. Just like an athlete, you get stronger in your "off season," you train, you build up your strength and resilience. If you read my book, ***My Beauty for Ashes,*** then you know that I didn't know anything about an off season. Instead of healing my heart, I was on to the next dysfunctional relationship. I never allowed myself an "off season" to heal and to listen to God. I thought what I needed was a new man in my life. Heal your heart first woman of God.

Survival Tip #7 - Forgive Yourself and Others

In order to be ready for your God-ordained husband, you must forgive. You cannot hold on to the spirit of offense because it is toxic. Forgiveness is required as a Christian, but many of us still struggle with this basic principle of our faith. Just as our Father in Heaven has forgiven us, we must forgive those who trespass against us. When you refuse to forgive, it hurts you, not the other person. Many times the person who we haven't forgiven has already moved on with their life and we find ourselves stuck in the past reliving the hurt. Let it go beautiful woman of God. Once I realized that hurt people hurt other people, I found it much easier to forgive. Many times we also struggle with forgiving ourselves.

For a very long time I struggled with forgiving myself. As a single mother I carried a lot of guilt and shame. Once I found out I was pregnant and I told my daughter's father, he cursed me out, told me he wanted nothing to do with it, and threatened me. I found it hard to forgive myself that I was in a situation where my daughter would not have a father in her life. I knew how painful it was when I lost my father at age 9. I didn't want my daughter to suffer that same emptiness and I blamed myself.

I accepted Jesus as my savior when I was 6 months pregnant and I was being exposed to his standard as a babe in Christ. I felt guilty walking into church week after week as an unwed pregnant mother and then single mother. The Lord had forgiven me, but I hadn't forgiven myself. I remember when my daughter was 3 years old, I attended a women's event sponsored by my former church. There was a young single mother who got up and shared her testimony about the shame she felt being around married Christian women. She broke down crying and then I started crying. I remember my friend Thyra coming over and putting her arms around us and telling us we had to forgive ourselves, that the Lord had forgiven us, but we had to do it too. In that circle as we held hands and prayed, I finally let go of the guilt and shame I had been carrying for far too long. Remember: there is no condemnation for those of us who are in Christ Jesus. Forgive yourself woman of God.

Survival Tip #8 – Get Rid of Mr. Right Now

Ok, here we go. Here is a very hard truth – many of you are not ready for God-ordained marriage because you are not free for God to bless you with your husband. If you are entertaining or dating someone you know is not your God-ordained husband, you must end it. Many of us are guilty of kicking it with Mr. Right Now. Let's be honest. You know without a shadow of a doubt he is not your husband, but you still text him, you still take his calls, you still allow him to take you out and for some of you, you still allow him to come over so you can "Netflix and chill." No, no, no, you are blocking your blessings woman of God.

Let me tell you that God had to deal with me in this area. I can't tell you how many Mr. Right Nows I have entertained in my past. I have never been confused about my future husband's character. After I was saved, God told me how he would treat me and showed me his character. However, time after time after time, I was hanging with Mr. Right Now because I wanted attention. Remember, I still had my baggage I hadn't unpacked so having Mr. Right Now text me that I was beautiful, take me out on dates, and whisper sweet nothings in my ear made me feel better. Mr. Right Now is a barrier to your promise woman of God.

Mr. Right Now is getting in the way of your Boaz finding you. You cannot have Mr. Right Now on the side to feed your loneliness. It doesn't work that way. Boaz is not going to come in and sweep you off your feet and then you tell Mr. Right Now that God has sent you your husband. God is not sending your husband when you are still entertaining counterfeit versions of his true blessing for you. You have to make a decision. You either trust God or you don't, you either believe he is going to give you the desires of your heart or you don't. You have to trust God that he can sustain you through this season, you have to know that he wants the best for you and you must know that he loves you too much to allow you to play with someone else's heart.

Survival Tip #9 - Know Your Worth as a Daughter of the King

Part of our issue is that we don't know who we are and that is why we settle. You are a daughter of the King, you are a queen, and you are precious in his sight. You need to see yourself the way God sees you. Once you know who you are and who you belong to, you will never settle for less than you deserve.

Once I truly knew who I was, there were certain things I would no longer entertain. I saw a quote on social media that stated, "The anointing attracts." Since I started walking in my purpose, I see that is so true. Yes, I had men approaching me prior to walking in my purpose, but this was so different. When you know your position in the Kingdom and your inheritance as a child of the most high God, something changes about your countenance. This anointing indeed attracts. You walk with authority and confidence. It is not arrogance or conceit, but it's knowing you truly are a daughter of the King. Men and certain behaviors that I would have considered entertaining two years ago, never again. Through my healing process and writing my first book, the Lord showed me why it was never going to work with my ex-boyfriends. He showed me where he was taking me and the standard and anointing of the man who will go with me. I don't have time for counterfeits. Too much is at stake. The way my anointing is set up, I just can't date anybody. Random dating, random texting, and random phone calls do not interest me. There is nothing "random" about my calling and anointing, and I don't have time to entertain anyone but my Boaz. I know who I am and what my Father wants for me.

What does your Heavenly Father say about you woman of God? How does he see you? He sees you as his child, he loves you, nothing can separate you from his love, you are precious to him, you are called, you are chosen, you are forgiven and your debt is paid through Christ Jesus. He wants you to trust him with your life and that means with all areas of your life, including who you will marry. Don't settle.

Survival Tip #10 – Never Settle

Many of us have been conditioned to settle. I have seen so many women and men who get tired of waiting on God and they have ended up in marriages that God did not ordain. Most led to divorce and with others they are simply roommates who have decided to just live separate lives under one roof and not truly as husband and wife.

One of the worst things you can do is settle for less than God's choice for you. The Lord gives us free will. We can choose to wait and prepare for God's best or we can take matters into our own hands. It saddens me when I am coaching someone who realizes they made a mistake and went ahead of God. I said it at the beginning of this book – marriage is serious business. You are entering into a legal contract and spiritual contract (covenant) when you take those vows for better or worse. I have never been divorced, but I know many people who had to go through that process and it's not fun.

I struggled with the subtitle of this book which described the book as a "Survival Guide," but that was the title the Lord gave me so I was obedient. I believe we were meant to thrive – not just survive. However, as a realist, I recognize that our society looks at singleness as a season we have to survive and that is so unfortunate. Marriage is not the point of when we have "arrived" in life, it is not the goal. Marriage is ordained by God for his glory and it is a blessing in his timing. God knows your deepest desires because he created you. I know many women who have no desire to be married because it's not a desire the Lord placed in their hearts. If you desire marriage, God is faithful and in his timing he will give you the desires of your heart.

Let's review everything you need in order to "survive" this season of singleness and prepare for your God-ordained marriage:

1. Seek God in order to discover your purpose
2. Get busy with your Father's business RIGHT NOW
3. Get out of driven to distraction mode now
4. Don't be fooled by the Counterfeit
5. Dump your baggage
6. Heal your heart
7. Forgive yourself and others
8. Get rid of Mr. Right Now
9. Know your worth as a daughter of the King
10. Don't settle

As a disciple of Jesus Christ, you have an important assignment in the Kingdom of God. You need to get busy on the mission about your Father's business. Like Ruth, you must move forward and not let the things that have happened in your past paralyze you from moving forward towards your future. Seek God, believe God, and trust God. You are his precious daughter and he loves you so much. If you leave the choice to him, he will send you your Boaz who will love you the way you deserve to be loved!

God is 100% faithful. Ask yourself, has he ever not come through, has he ever forsaken you or lied to you? If he made you this promise, he is faithful and will give it to you. Beautiful woman of God, the promise and the wait are worth it when God shows up with your blessing. Prepare while you wait and watch him show up and show out!!!

Praying for Your Boaz

Beautiful woman of God, it is so important that you begin praying for your Boaz now. As a wife it will be your call to cover your husband in prayer daily. You need to start that disciplined practice right now – not after the wedding. The enemy hates God-ordained marriages and he is already forming weapons in advance to destroy your marriage. Your future marriage is a threat to the enemy's agenda. Remember his agenda never changes: he came to steal, kill, and destroy. He doesn't want to see Godly marriages thrive. A couple ordained by God and on fire for their purpose and destiny will advance the kingdom of God. Your marriage is a ministry and it will produce fruit. The enemy does not want to see that. The Lord placed it in my spirit in 2016 to begin praying for my husband.

I suggest that you purchase a journal where you will write to your future husband. I have quotes, scriptures, and prayers for my Boaz that I write in my journal. Here is a sample entry from my prayer journal. Begin your journal today by writing in the next section and then create your own journal. I think the greatest gift you can give your husband on your wedding day is this journal. He will know that even before you ever met, you were praying for him, his purpose, and the ministry of your marriage.

Dear Future Husband,

Today I pray that you are walking boldly in your purpose. I know that the call on your life is a great one and I pray that God has granted you the wisdom and tenacity to step into everything he has called you to be. I pray that today you are free from distractions and that any weapon that the enemy tries to form will be cancelled. I pray God's covering over you. I am working on preparing myself to be the best wife I can be to you. I just want to be a blessing to you and fulfill the purpose and destiny that is on the ministry of our marriage.

I love you,

Your future wife!

Prayer Journal

Begin writing entries to your future husband. Write whatever the Lord places on your heart. Do this for at least 7 days and then start your own separate journal to give to him.

Day 1

Day 2

Day 3

Day 4

Day 5

Day 6

Day 7

Reflections from the Author

It's funny that I had no idea that the Lord's plan was that I author several books. Well, that's not completely true. One day I was at lunch with my friend Jeniffer who has a prophetic gift and has prophesized about several things in my life and casually said to me, "You know this is not your only book, right?" I just gave her that "look," which meant I knew the Lord was speaking through her, but I wasn't ready to receive it at that time. Originally, I thought the Lord was calling me to share my testimony (**My Beauty for Ashes**) and that was it. However, one day while I was at lunch, just as Jeniffer had said, he downloaded the name of this book, chapter outline, and the cover. So, I said, "Ok Lord, I guess I am writing another book."

It's funny that in the last year I haven't really been thinking about marriage the way I used to. The Lord has completely transformed and renewed my mind about the purpose of marriage and at the same time changed the desire. Yes, I still have a strong desire to be married, but it's not my frequent thought or my every thought. I am so on fire for my purpose that it has shifted to the back of my mind. I never thought I would say that. I know that Boaz is out there walking in his purpose, on fire for what God is calling him to do as well. God is the ultimate matchmaker and when the time is right, he is going to see to it that we are going to be in the right place at the right time.

I started writing this book in March 2017 shortly after **My Beauty for Ashes** was released and I completed several chapters as the Lord spoke to me. Then for 3 months he was silent. Then all of a sudden he started downloading again so I continued writing. He dropped in my spirit that I needed to finish this book so of course I was obedient. He started to give me more intimate details about my Boaz. He told me he was moving me from my place of pain to my purpose and destiny like Ruth. He told me that my Boaz was going to be a major upgrade from any relationship I had ever experienced and that he was going to find me smack dead in the middle of my purpose. He has given me vivid visions of my husband and I talking about this book at speaking engagements. We will be passionately pursuing our purposes for the Kingdom together. My Boaz is my purpose mate.

I allowed the Lord to speak through me and these were the words he placed on my heart to encourage you. I pray that this book blessed you as it blessed me through the writing process. I have such a heart for the single Christian woman. I understand the societal pressure to be "booed up" and in a relationship when you are waiting on God's promise. I also know the heartbreak of being in a relationship God did not ordain.

My prayer is that you will not take matters into your own hands, and that you will fully walk in purpose while preparing yourself for the love you deserve. Please trust God to give you the desires of your heart.

His promise will be worth the wait.

About the Author

Tonia is first and foremost a chosen disciple of Jesus Christ. She is a best-selling author, life coach, and speaker. She is also the founder of Ruth and Boaz in the Meantime Ministries and is passionate about Christians discovering and walking in their purpose.

She holds a Bachelor's degree in Education from State University of New York, College at Old Westbury, a Master's degree in Communication Studies from California State University, Los Angeles, an HR Management certificate from The University of California, Irvine, and holds a Life Coach certification from Life Coach Training Institute, accredited by the International Association of Certified Coaches.

Follow her at:

Instagram: @RuthandBoazmeantimeministries

Twitter: @ToniaShalel

Facebook: @RuthandBoazinthemeantimeministry

YouTube: @ToniaShalel

Find us online at http://www.toniashalel.com

To book Tonia for your next event, email:
toniashalel@gmail.com

www.ingramcontent.com/pod-product-compliance
Lightning Source LLC
LaVergne TN
LVHW051156080426
835508LV00021B/2669